WOMEN EMPOWERMENT

VOLUME 2, ISSUE 2 OF BRILLOPEDIA

S. NANDHINI

Contents

Preface

"Start writing, no matter what. The water does not flow until the faucet is turned on".

-Louis L'Amour

Hundreds of students and professors are contributing their work to Brillopedia, we are here to provide ample information about Law and Contemporary issues. Our aim is to provide a platform for today's generation to express their views and ideas on law and contemporary law.

Author

CHAPTER ONE

Abstract

Women empowerment is a commonly heard word in recent days. Every woman has many responsibilities. They must have freedom in their lives. Women are the backbone of their families. Every woman should be educationally and financially independent. If they are educated, they can proceed to a job and they can earn for their needs. In that sense, they can be financially independent. Every woman has the right to acquire property from her in-law's house and her parent's house. Property not only provides status to the women but also guarantees securities. Art- 21 A says about the right to education for both genders. The state shall provide free & compulsory education between six to fourteen years of age. Education is must for all human beings. The major problem in India is domestic violence. To prevent these kinds of violations against women, the government of India enacted much legislation such as "The protection of women from violence Act,2005" and "The indecent Representation of women (Prohibition) Act "and so on.

"Empowered women

Empower women"

CHAPTER TWO

Introduction

Every woman is a beautiful creation of God. This is so fact because great personalities are born from the womb of women. Every woman has many responsibilities towards their family as men. In this, we shall discuss the possibilities and achievements as well as obstacles and challenges faced by women.

Meaning

Here, women's empowerment is made up of two words. women and empowerment. Empowerment refers to giving power to someone or giving authority to someone. And also women empowerment means power in the hands of women.

Importance of women empowerment:

1. Every woman must have the freedom that every human deserves not only for being able to decide on her own but to live without restrictions.

2. Every woman is considered the backbone of their family.

3. women are multitaskers, they can do all kinds of work without getting tired or without complaining.

Eg: Managing the work, taking care of the house, being able to live productively etc.

4. women are falsely blamed as feminists for showing up their strength or voicing out the bad.

5. Every year 8th March is declared as International women's day to promote women's participation in society. International Women's day is declared by UNO.

CHAPTER THREE

Need for women empowerment

As we know women's abilities to make their choices on their own had been denied once, changes took place only when the mindset of the women who struggled was broken and struggles were turned into achievements.

1. By empowering women we not only achieve gender equality but also raise the status of women.

2. we train women to face the challenge on their own. We also make them aware of their rights, their needs and wants etc.

3. Empowering a woman is like teaching a child to walk. It is as necessary and as important to teach a child to walk and so is empowering.

4. Empowering does not mean degrading men or lifting the women who are in the dark.

To do so we need a woman to attain a set of goals like good health, proper education, employment, freedom, a judgment-less society, appreciating and supportive parents, motivating husbands and in-laws, violence-free marriage etc.

Women have to grow up mentally, physically and most importantly knowledgeable in every stage of life.

CHAPTER FOUR

Educational rights

Nowadays education is a must for every woman. If a woman is educated she will be aware of women's rights and she will come to know how to fight against violence.

Article 21A of the Indian Constitution deals with the Right to Education for both genders. The age between six to fourteen is the age to get compulsory education and the state government provides free education as well.

Education is for all human beings. It should not be snatched away from women. She has every right to get an education. Major heart-wrenching incidents and accidents happen only because of illiteracy.

When compared to urban, rural has the lowest literacy rate in India. Compared to men, women in India do not get a proper education. We all know women cannot be blamed for their education it is the ill-treated society or narrow-minded parents that has to take the blame.

Women in this era are creating new records breaking the stereotypes and being able to voice out without fear of judgement. This happened because of the right education. So, education is a must and she deserves to be educated without questioning.

CHAPTER FIVE

Domestic violence in marriage for women

Domestic violence is a major problem in India. The married woman has all rights in her groom's house. As per in Hindu Succession Act 1956, Every woman has the right to get back their dowry from her in-law's house.

If women's rights get violated, they can give complain and file a case under section 19, The Protection of Women from Domestic Violence, 2005.

After divorce woman has the right to take her child in her custody without issuing legal papers. If a woman is not interested in giving birth to a child, and if she gets pregnant without her interest, she can abort without getting permission in her law's house and she should abort within 24 weeks under the Medical Termination of Pregnancy Act,1971.

Women have the right to file a case, if their in-laws trouble her about dowry, they can file a case under Dowry Prohibition Act,1961.

With the help of this Act and women being aware of the law and orders dowry problems have decreased these days, on the other hand, it still prevails and is not fully abolished.

CHAPTER SIX

Property Rights

As per law, every woman has the property right. According to Hindu Succession Act, 1956 Every woman has the right to get property from her parents. She has also the right to acquire property from her in-law's house.

Property not only provides status to the women but also guarantees security. Women being exploited in many ways can live a safe and secure life by claiming their property.

As property rights mean ownership women are not any less to have or acquire one. So it is vital that women have to get their property to live in an exploited society.

CHAPTER SEVEN

Constitutional provisions

Article 14 and 21 of the Indian constitution provides the Right to Equality and the Right to life and personal liberty as fundamental rights to its citizen without discrimination.

Indecent Representation of Women (Prohibition) Act1986:

The Indecent Representation of Women (Prohibition) Act was enacted in 1986. The purpose of the act is to prohibit indecent representation of women through advertisements, paintings, photography etc.

Section 6 of the Act deals with punishment for an offence made by a person.

Women change the world:

1. Women as already said a multitasker, manages households and contributes to the nation's development in many possible ways.

2. Women being aware of their rights are fighting against injustice.

3. They contribute equally as men but get paid lesser than men.

4. Though there are lots of ups and downs in a women's life she never gives up. Not only for her future but she also paves way for the upcoming generation.

5. Being said by the world the women only become responsible for the success of the family now women are achieving heights and fear none.

6. we had also seen Queen like Rani Lakshmi bai . she is a great warrior. and she gave hope to the upcoming women during her period.

7. women not only take care of the house, but they also promote, project, and organize the whole world.

CHAPTER EIGHT

Case study

Vishaka vs state

The first thing that comes to our mind when we get to see or face sexual harassment at the workplace is Vishaka's case. It is an important landmark case related to sexual harassment in the workplace.

Background of the case

A girl named Banwari Devi from Rajasthan worked in a women's development Project. This project was initiated by the government. The main aim of the project was to abolish child marriage. The Banwari Devi's task is to prevent child marriage.

In Rajasthan, there is a village in that village there lived a family called Ram Karan guru. He arranged a marriage for her minor daughter who is less than one year. Banwari Devi notices this and tries to convince the family to stop this marriage but the family did not agree.

5th May 1992 was the date set for the marriage luckily DSP of such a village finds out and stops the marriage. The very next day the Karan family made the child marry and no police came to stop them.

As Ram Karan is the most popular and influential person and nobody was against it. Later Ram Karan and his family came to know about Banwari Devi's attempt of stopping the marriage. Ram Karan wants to take revenge on Banwari Devi.

Banwari Devi lost her job because of ram Karan. In the motive of taking revenge on Banwari Devi, the members of the Ram Karan family members have raped her.

Even in medical examination, it was not mentioned. Despite all these, she files a case against them. But MLA is very known to Ram Karan's Family and with the support of MLA he comes out not proven guilty. Many women activists come to know of this issue. And they file a PIL in front of the court.

Judgement

The fundamental right under Art 14, Art 15, and Art 21 of the Indian constitution were violated in this case.

Sexual harassment has been deeply defined in this case. If there is no physical contact between them but if verbal abuse presents in it, that is also referred to as sexual harassment. Sharing porn videos with others is also known as sexual harassment.

In this judgement, the court has mentioned specially, "The sexual harassment and Right to work with dignity will also include in gender equality".

The guidelines which were given in this case were named "vishaka guidelines

1. Employeer responsibility is to give healthy work conditions to women.

2. If any mistakes happened in the workplace, immediate actions must be taken.

3. Redressal committee should be formed in every workplace. In this committee, half of the members should be women. There should be a woman-headed committee.

CHAPTER NINE

Conclusion & Suggestions

<u>**Suggestions**</u>

1. Every woman should feel inside them, that they are empowered.
2. No man should dominate women. They should give respect to the words of women.

<u>**Conclusion**</u>

Here I conclude that nowadays every women's socially, educationally, politically, and economically free. Every parent should provide better education for girls. In our society, peoples should avoid child marriage and a non-educational system for women. This will help women to come forward.